BRITISH RAILWAYS STEAMING ON THE EX-LNER LINES

Volume Two

Compiled by

PETER HANDS & COLIN RICHARDS

DEFIANT PUBLICATIONS
190 Yoxall Road,
Shirley, Solihull,
West Midlands

Printed on behalf of Richard Netherwood Ltd by Gorenjski Tisk, Yugolslavia

CURRENT STEAM PHOTOGRAPH ALBUMS AVAILABLE
FROM DEFIANT PUBLICATIONS

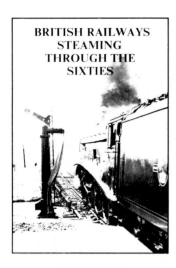

BRITISH RAILWAYS STEAMING THROUGH THE SIXTIES

VOLUME 11
A4 size - Hardback. 100 pages
-180 b/w photographs.
£10.95 + £1.00 postage.
ISBN 0 946857 24 5.

BRITISH RAILWAYS STEAMING THROUGH THE SIXTIES

VOLUME 12
A4 size - Hardback. 100 pages
-182 b/w photographs.
£11.95 + £1.00 postage.
ISBN 0 946857 27 X.

BRITISH RAILWAYS STEAMING THROUGH THE SIXTIES

VOLUME 13
A4 size - Hardback. 100 pages
-182 b/w photographs.
£11.95 + £1.00 postage.
ISBN 0 946857 33 4.

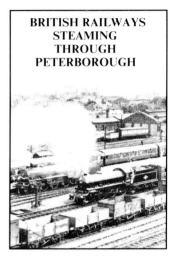

BRITISH RAILWAYS STEAMING THROUGH PETERBOROUGH

A4 size - Hardback. 100 pages
-163 b/w photographs.
£10.95 + £1.00 postage.
ISBN 0 946857 26 1.

BRITISH RAILWAYS STEAMING ON THE WESTERN REGION

VOLUME 3
A4 size - Hardback. 100 pages
-179 b/w photographs.
£10.95 + £1.00 postage.
ISBN 0 946857 25 3.

BRITISH RAILWAYS STEAMING ON THE WESTERN REGION

IN PREPARATION

VOLUME 4

BRITISH RAILWAYS STEAMING ON THE SOUTH COAST

A4 size - Hardback. 100 pages
-182 b/w photographs.
£11.95 + £1.00 postage.
ISBN 0 946857 29 6.

BRITISH RAILWAYS STEAMING ON THE SOUTHERN REGION

IN PREPARATION

VOLUME 3

BRITISH RAILWAYS STEAMING ON THE LONDON MIDLAND REGION

VOLUME 3
A4 size - Hardback. 100 pages
-181 b/w photographs.
£11.95 + £1.00 postage.
ISBN 0 946857 28 8.

BRITISH RAILWAYS STEAMING ON THE LONDON MIDLAND REGION

IN PREPARATION

VOLUME 4

BRITISH RAILWAYS STEAMING ON THE EX-LNER LINES

VOLUME 2
A4 size - Hardback. 100 pages
-187 b/w photographs.
£11.95 + £1.00 postage.
ISBN 0 946857 34 2.

BRITISH RAILWAYS STEAMING ON THE SCOTTISH REGION

IN PREPARATION

VOLUME 1

CURRENT STEAM PHOTOGRAPH ALBUMS AVAILABLE
FROM DEFIANT PUBLICATIONS

VOLUME 1
A4 size - Hardback. 100 pages
-180 b/w photographs.
£8.95 + £1.00 postage.
ISBN 0 946857 12 1.

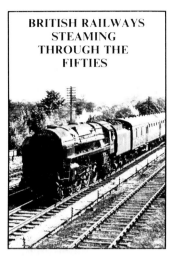

VOLUME 2
A4 size - Hardback. 100 pages
-180 b/w photographs.
£8.95 + £1.00 postage.
ISBN 0 946857 13 X.

VOLUME 3
A4 size - Hardback. 100 pages
-180 b/w photographs.
£9.95 + £1.00 postage.
ISBN 0 946857 16 4.

VOLUME 4
A4 size - Hardback. 100 pages
-180 b/w photographs.
£9.95 + £1.00 postage.
ISBN 0 946857 17 2.

VOLUME 5
A4 size - Hardback. 100 pages
-180 b/w photographs.
£9.95 + £1.00 postage.
ISBN 0 946857 22 9.

VOLUME 6
A4 size - Hardback. 100 pages
-180 b/w photographs.
£9.95 + £1.00 postage.
ISBN 0 946857 23 7.

VOLUME 7
A4 size - Hardback. 100 pages
-180 b/w photographs.
£11.95 + £1.00 postage.
ISBN 0 946857 31 8.

VOLUME 8
A4 size - Hardback. 100 pages
-180 b/w photographs.
£11.95 + £1.00 postage.
ISBN 0 946857 32 6.

BRITISH RAILWAYS
STEAMING
THROUGH THE
FIFTIES

IN
PREPARATION

BRITISH RAILWAYS
STEAMING
THROUGH THE
FIFTIES

IN
PREPARATION

BRITISH RAILWAYS
STEAMING
THROUGH CREWE,
DONCASTER,
EASTLEIGH AND
SWINDON

IN
PREPARATION

BRITISH RAILWAYS
STEAMING
FROM ST. PANCRAS
TO ST. ENOCH

IN
PREPARATION

VOLUME 9

VOLUME 10

OTHER TITLES AVAILABLE FROM DEFIANT PUBLICATIONS

PRICES VARY FROM £1 to £3.80 INCLUDING POSTAGE

WHAT HAPPENED TO STEAM
Volume One
THE GREAT WESTERN
2800 Class 2-8-0's
&
R.O.D. Class 2-8-0's

WHAT HAPPENED TO STEAM

This series of booklets, 50 in all, is designed to inform the reader of the allocations, re-allocations and dates of withdrawal of steam locomotives during their last years of service. From 1957 onwards and finally where the locomotives concerned were stored and subsequently scrapped.

BR STEAM SHED ALLOCATIONS

This series lists all individual steam locomotives based at the different parent depots of B.R. from January 1957 until each depot either closed to steam or closed completely. An attractive book binder is available for this thirteen book series.

B.R. STEAM SHED ALLOCATIONS
Part One
WESTERN REGION SHEDS
81A Old Oak Common · 81F Oxford
82A Bristol (Bath Road) · 82F Weymouth
83A Newton Abbot · 83G Penzance

WHAT HAPPENED TO STEAM
THE L.N.E.R.
B1 4-6-0's.

WHAT HAPPENED TO STEAM
THE SOUTHERN
H15, N15, 'KING ARTHURS' S15
& 'LORD NELSON' 4-6-0's.
G16 4-8-0 TANKS.
H16 4-6-2 TANKS.

B. R. STEAM SHED ALLOCATIONS
Part Four
EASTERN REGION SHEDS
30A Stratford · 30F Parkeston
31A Cambridge · 31E Bury St Edmunds
32A New ... 'th Constable
33A ...
34. Kings ...
35A New England · ...

B. R. STEAM SHED ALLOCATIONS
Part Five
EASTERN REGION SHEDS
36A Doncaster · 36E Retford
38A Colwick · 38E Woodford Halse
39A Gorton
40A Lincoln · 40F Boston
41A Darnall (Sheffield)

WHAT HAPPENED TO STEAM
THE LNW 0-8-0's
Nos. 48895-49674
L & Y TANK CLASSES -
Nos. 50636-51546
&
L & Y 0-6-0's Nos. 52089-52529
Volume Forty-Seven

WHAT HAPPENED TO STEAM
THE
LONDON MIDLAND
2F & 3F
0-6-0 TANKS
Nos. 47160-9 & 47200-681
VOLUME FORTY-FIVE

B. R. STEAM SHED ALLOCATIONS
Part Six
NORTH EASTERN REGION SHEDS
50A York · 50G Whitby
51A Darlington · 51L Thornaby
52A Gateshead · 52F Blyth

B. R. STEAM SHED ALLOCATIONS
Part Seven
NORTH EASTERN REGION SHEDS
53A Hull (Dairycoates) · 53E Goole
54A Sunderland · 54D Consett
55A Leeds (Holbeck) · 55G Huddersfield
56A Wakefield · 56G Bradford (Hammerton St.)

WHAT HAPPENED TO STEAM
THE L.N.E.R.
V2 2-6-2's
Nos. 60800-983
VOLUME EIGHT

WHAT HAPPENED TO STEAM
THE B.R.
CLASS 4 4-6-0's & 2-6-0's
Nos. 75000-79 & 76000-114

B. R. STEAM SHED ALLOCATIONS
Part Eight
SCOTTISH REGION SHEDS
60A Inverness · 60E Forres
61A Kittybrewster · 61C Keith
62A Thornton Junction · 62C Dunfermline
63A Perth · 63D Oban
64A St. Margarets (Edinburgh) · 64G Hawick
65A Eastfield (Glasgow) · 65J Fort William
66A Polmadie (Glasgow) · 66D Greenock (Ladyburn)
67A Corkerhill (Glasgow) · 67D Ardrossan
68A Carlisle (Kingmoor) · 68E Carlisle (Canal)
St. Rollox Works

B. R. STEAM SHED ALLOCATIONS
Part Nine
SOUTHERN REGION SHEDS
70A Nine Elms · 70H Ryde (I.O.W.)
71A Eastleigh · 71J Highbridge
72A Exmouth Jct. · 72F Wadebridge
73A Stewarts Lane · 73E Faversham
74A Ashford · 74E St Leonards
75A Brighton · 75F Tunbridge Wells

WHAT HAPPENED TO STEAM
Volume Twenty Eight
THE
L.M.S.
8F 2-8-0's
&
Somerset and Dorset
7F 2-8-0's

WHAT HAPPENED TO STEAM
THE GREAT WESTERN
15xx, 34xx, 84xx, & 94xx
series of
0-6-0 's
PANNIER TANKS
VOLUME THIRTY ONE

B. R. STEAM SHED ALLOCATIONS
Part Eleven
LONDON MIDLAND REGION SHEDS
8A Edge Hill (Liverpool) · 8E Brunswick (Liverpool)
9A Longsight (Manchester) · 9G Northwich
10A Springs Branch Wigan · 10D Sutton Oak
11A Carnforth · 11E Lancaster (Green Ayre)
12A Carlisle (Upperby) · 12C Workington

B. R. STEAM SHED ALLOCATIONS
Part Twelve
LONDON MIDLAND REGION SHEDS
14A Cricklewood · 14C St. Albans
15A Wellingborough · 15D Bedford
16A Nottingham · 16C Mansfield
17A Derby · 17D Rowsley
18A Toton · 18D Staveley (Barrow Hill)
19A Sheffield (Grimesthorpe) · 19C Canklow

ACKNOWLEDGEMENTS

Grateful thanks are extended to the following contributors of photographs not only for their use in this book but for their kind patience and long term loan of negatives/photographs whilst this book was being compiled.

T. R. AMOS
TAMWORTH

W. BOYDEN
BEXHILL**

L. BROWNHILL
BRIERLEY HILL

R. S. CARPENTER
BIRMINGHAM

S. GRADIDGE
CHALFONT ST. GILES

R. W. HINTON
GLOUCESTER

F. HORNBY
NORTH CHEAM

ERIC LIGHT
TICKHILL

STUART PITCHFORTH
SANDAL

B. RANDS
WESTON-SUPER-MARE

J. SCHATZ
LITTLETHORPE

DEREK SINGLETON
***

R. TURNER
SHEFFIELD

B. J. ASHWORTH
PENTYRCH

B. W. L. BROOKSBANK
LONDON

R. BUTTERFIELD
MIRFIELD

KEN ELLIS
SWINDON

PETER HAY
HOVE

H. L. HOLLAND
ST. CATHERINES, ONTARIO, CANADA

A. C. INGRAM
WISBECH

A. F. NISBET
BRACKLEY

J. H. PRICE
*

E. L. RIVETT
ARUNDEL

K. L. SEAL
ANDOVERSFORD

M. S. STOKES
MARPLE

KIT WINDLE
LOWER BREDBURY

R. BARTLETT
SAFETY BAY
WESTERN AUSTRALIA

N. L. BROWNE
ALDERSHOT

P. CANE
HARPENDEN

A. N. H. GLOVER
BIRMINGHAM

MIKE HIGSON
THE SMOKEBOX

D. K. JONES
MOUNTAIN ASH

LES PERRIN
BOSTON

N. E. PREEDY
HUCCLECOTE

M. RUTTER
BOWER GRANGE

G. W. SHARPE
BARNSLEY

A. SWAIN
WEMBLEY

J. WRAITHMELL
MIRFIELD

* Courtesy of the A. C. Ingram collection. ** Courtesy of the Frank Hornby collection.

*** From the Preston Whiteley collection (Kendall) courtesy of David Alexander, Morecambe.

Front Cover — Steam streams gently from the safety valves of a highly polished LNER B1 Class 4-6-0 No 61179, a 34A Kings Cross inmate, as it heads a down 'Butlins Express', complete with headboard, through Spalding station on 25th August 1962.

(T.R. Amos)

ISBN 0 946857 34 2

© P. B. HANDS/C. RICHARDS 1991
FIRST PUBLISHED 1991

INTRODUCTION

BRITISH RAILWAYS STEAMING ON THE EX-LNER LINES — Volume Two is the third book to concentrate on the now British Railways tracks and locomotives once owned or influenced by this once great railway company. The authors hope the reader will enjoy the diverse variety of locomotives and locations within the pages of this album.

The 'BR Steaming' books are designed to give the ordinary, everyday steam photographic enthusiast of the 1950's and 1960's a chance to participate in and give pleasure to others whilst recapturing the twilight days of steam.

Apart from the 1950's and 1960's series, individual regional albums like this one will be produced from time to time. Wherever possible, no famous names will be found nor will photographs which have been published before be used. Nevertheless, the content and quality of the majority of photographs used will be second to none.

BRITISH RAILWAYS STEAMING ON THE EX-LNER LINES — Volume Two is divided into three chapters covering the Eastern, North Eastern and Scottish Regions of British Railways from 1948-67, by which time allocated steam had finished on all three regions. Unless otherwise stated all locomotives are of LNER origin.

The purists may argue that not all of the locations and locomotives included in this album are of pure LNER origin. The authors have included some photographs of areas taken over by the BR Regions and of locomotives constructed after nationalisation in 1948 but allocated to the same. The authors have also attempted to vary the locations as much as possible but some areas of greater interest e.g. Doncaster, Edinburgh and York etc., have been given more coverage than others.

The majority of the photographs used in this album have been contributed by readers of Peter Hands series of booklets entitled "What Happened to Steam" & "BR Steam Shed Allocations" and from readers of the earlier "BR Steaming Through the Sixties" albums. In normal circumstances these may have been hidden from the public eye forever.

The continuation of the "BR Steaming" series etc., depends upon you the reader. If you feel you have suitable material of BR steam locomotives between 1948-1968 and wish to contribute them towards the series and other future publications please contact either:

Peter Hands,
190 Yoxall Road,
Shirley, Solihull,   OR
West Midlands B90 3RN

Colin Richards
28 Kendrick Close,
Damson Parkway, Solihull,
West Midlands B92 0QD

Peter Hands

CONTENTS

EASTERN REGION

	PAGES		PAGES
NAMEPLATES	5	Kings Cross	12/22/35
		Kings Lynn	10
Beccles	33		
Boston	8/23	Langwith Junction	33/36
Cambridge	15/17/20/37	Liverpool Street	18
Canklow	22	Lowestoft	13
Colwick	31		
		Manningtree	26
Doncaster	8/14/24/32/34	March	12/21/35
Essendine	27	Mildenhall	14
Firsby	24		
Frodingham	26	North Weald	30
		Norwich	7/11
Grantham	27/36		
Grassthorpe	13	Peterborough	23/29/30
Grimsby	10	Sandy	31
		Sheffield	9/19/29
Hackney Downs	37	Shoeburyness	25
Harwich	20	Spalding	17/28 & Front Cover
Hatfield	19	Spital Bridge	9/16
Hitchin	18	Staveley	16/34
Hornsey	7/15/21	Stratford	6/25
Immingham	11/28	Whitlingham	32

NORTH EASTERN REGION

Alston	59	Newcastle	43
		Newport	40
Bedlington	52	Normanton	48/62
Blyth	43	North Blyth	61
Borough Gardens	46		
Bradford	54	Royston	67
Bridlington	49		
		Saltburn	63
Consett	51	Scarborough	63/66
Copley Hill	55	Selby	41/58
Crofton	66	Sowerby Bridge	50
Darlington	42/47/52/56/62	Stockton	45
		Stourton	64
Farnley Junction	42	Sunderland	61
Gateshead	53/60		
		Thornaby	57
Halifax	51	Tyne Dock	64
Hartlepool	44		
Heaton	56	Wakefield	39/41/44/53/55/58
Hull	48/65	Wansbeck	45
		West Hartlepool	46/49/65
Leeds	39/50/57/59	Whitby	60
Low Moor	67	York	38/40/47/54 & Rear Cover Bottom

SCOTTISH REGION

Aberdeen	70/86	Ibrox	91
Alloa	82/89	Inverurie	74/77
Alva	81		
Arbroath	84	Kipps	80/81/94
		Kittybrewster	76/78/84/92/94
Ballater	86		
Bathgate	93	Langholm	85
Bishopbriggs	79	Longtown	96
Bo'Ness	89		
Bridge of Orchy	72	Mallaig	74/83
Burntisland	95	Monessie Gorge	69
		Newport-on-Tay	70
Carlisle (Canal)	82		
		Polmont	69
Dundee	73/75/76		
Dunfermline	68	St. Boswells	90
		St. Margarets	73/85/96 & Rear Cover Top
Eastfield (Glasgow)	71/78		
Edinburgh	71/88/92	Seafield	91
Elgin	80	South Leith	79
		Stonehaven	72/88
Fort William	87		
		Tayport	90
Hawick	75/93	Thornton Jct.	83/87/95
Haymarket	77		

NAMEPLATES — MEMORIES OF THE LONDON NORTH EASTERN RAILWAY.

1) Nameplate of A4 Class 4-6-2 No 60026 *Miles Beevor.* (S. Gradidge)

2) Nameplate of A2/3 Class 4-6-2 No 60500 *Edward Thompson.* (S. Gradidge)

3) A collection of famous headboards at Grantham shed 3rd October 1954. (R. Butterfield)

4) Newsham station NER on 13th June 1956. Closed during 1964. (F. Hornby)

5) Warning notice at Keith Town station Sc.R 19th June 1958. (N. L. Browne)

6)   The living, the dying and the dead are assembled together outside Stratford Works in March 1959. The 'living' are Hill J19 Class 0-6-0 No 64666 and Worsdell J15 Class 0-6-0 No 65447 (the latter for only one month longer). The 'dying' is Holden J68 Class 0-6-0T No 68638 (latterly of 34F Grantham) withdrawn this same month. The 'dead' is an unidentified pile of scrap in a wagon behind No 68638. (M.F. Higson)

7) A fine array of elevated upper quadrant semaphore signals overlook the multiple tracks at Hornsey on the East Coast Main Line, four miles away from Kings Cross terminus in June 1962. LNER A4 Class 4-6-2 No 60021 *Wild Swan* (34A Kings Cross) speeds towards the extensive carriage sidings in the distance with a down Anglo-Scottish express. (A.F. Nisbet)

8) L1 Class 2-6-4T No 67730 stands in the yard at its home shed of 32A Norwich next to an unidentified English Electric Type 3 diesel on 10th May 1961. No 67730 had been based at 30A Stratford for many years before being drafted to Norwich in December 1960. It returned to Stratford shed in February 1962 and was withdrawn from there six months later. Scrapping came at Darlington Works in October 1962. (N.E. Preedy)

9)   A fine panoramic view taken at Boston in Lincolnshire on 11th June 1956. With safety valves lifting B1 Class 4-6-0 No 61159, from 40B Immingham, passes Boston locoshed and a duet of steam engines whilst in charge of a Kings Cross to Cleethorpes express. The bulk of the allocation at the shed, coded 40F, were of LNER origin supplemented by a large number of LMR Class 4 'Flying Pig' 2-6-0's. The shed closed in January 1964. (Les Perrin)

10)   A magnificent portrait of Thompson A2/2 Class 4-6-2 No 60501 *Cock O' The North*, a 50A York locomotive, outshopped at Doncaster during the 1950's. *Cock O' The North* is a rebuild of a Gresley P2 Class 2-8-2 (rebuilt in 1944) No 2001. The small smoke deflectors attempt to shield the rather ugly rimless chimney. Withdrawn from York shed in February, it was cut up at Doncaster Works two months later. (Stuart Pitchforth)

11)   Although of Midland Railway heritage and coded 16B in 1948 under British Railways ownership, Spital Bridge shed in Peterborough became the property of the Eastern Region in 1950 adopting the code of 35C. On 1st February 1958 the code changed for a final time to 31F. Seen outside its home in 1959 is B1 Class 4-6-0 No 61096 which was later transferred to 31B March in January 1960. (A.C. Ingram)

12)   Another location of London Midland origin which became the property of the Eastern Region is Sheffield (Midland) station. On 3rd September 1966 a crowd has gathered on a platform to admire a rarity in the shape of 55C Farnley Junction LMS *Jubilee* 4-6-0 No 45562 *Alberta* which is leaving the station with the last summer Saturday Bradford to Poole holiday working. Decidedly the event of the week at Sheffield (Midland). (M.S. Stokes)

13) The former Great Eastern Railway station at Kings Lynn was joined to the M & GN Joint station at South Lynn by a two coach shuttle service which met most trains on the M & GN, rather like the station bus. It saved the Kings Lynn people a two mile trek from South Lynn, the M & GN passing south of the town. On 4th April 1956 it is being worked by C12 Class 4-4-2T No 67386, seen here passing 31C Kings Lynn shed. (Peter Hay)

14) A group of workmen and a lorry have their progress impeded by a level crossing gate at Grimsby Docks on Thursday 28th September 1961. B1 Class 4-6-0 No 61121 (36A Doncaster) leaves the Docks station in a cloud of smoke and steam and heads for Cleethorpes. This view from the Royal Hotel shows the level crossing which is reputed to have been the busiest in the world, handling some 900 train movements a day. (J.H. Price)

15) A fine 1957 panoramic view of the yard, coaling plant and running shed at 32A Norwich. In the extreme left of the picture is K3 Class 2-6-0 No 61981, a resident of the shed. Immediately behind No 61981 is D16 Class 4-4-0 No 62562 a visitor from 32G Melton Constable. Between the concrete coaling plant and the shed are two unidentified BR *Britannia* Class 4-6-2's. Norwich closed to steam in September 1962. (R.S. Carpenter)

16) A 41H Staveley G.C. Thompson rebuild 01 Class 2-8-0 No 63646 is noted in steam in the shed yard at 40B Immingham on 28th April 1963. Originally built by the Great Central Railway as an 04 in 1918, No 63646 was rebuilt in September 1945. Transferred to 41J Langwith Junction after the closure of Staveley G.C. shed in June 1965, it only survived in service for a further month before being condemned. (F. Hornby)

17)   Sunlight reflects through the glass panels in the magnificent overall roof at Kings Cross terminus on a summer's day in 1960. Nobody, apart from the photographer, takes an iota of notice of 36A Doncaster based A1 Class 4-6-2 No 60114 *W.P. Allen* as it quietly simmers after arriving with an up express. Passengers of all ages mill round the platforms in the dress of the day. (Stuart Pitchforth)

18)   Its tender laden with coal supplies D16/3 'Claud Hamilton' Class 4-4-0 No 62615 awaits the arrival of its fireman as he strides towards the locomotive prior to it departing from the yard of its home shed at 31B March in September 1957. No 62615 is a rebuild of an earlier D16/2 Class locomotive, having a round-topped boiler. It was withdrawn from March shed in October 1958. (A.C. Ingram)

12

19)   The Norfolk & Suffolk Joint Line was home to a shuttle service between Lowestoft, Gorleston and Yarmouth (South Town) until 1970. All sorts of local engines were used over the years. Here it is with C12 Class 4-4-2T No 67366, from 32D Yarmouth (South Town) shed, in charge on 6th April 1956. No 67366 is passing the Lowestoft carriage sidings and the Eastern Coachworks, birthplace of many buses. (Peter Hay)

20)   Gresley A4 Class 4-6-2 No 60009 *Union of South Africa,* from far off 61B Aberdeen (Ferryhill), its white exhaust highlighted by a weak sun, approaches Grassthorpe Crossing, north of Newark, on the East Coast Main Line with the northbound journey of the RCTS/SLS 'Jubilee Requiem' railtour from Kings Cross to Newcastle and return on 24th October 1964. (K.L. Seal)

21) Although Spring is on the horizon the East Anglian frosts keep a wintry look at Mildenhall on 2nd April 1956 and the trees are bare as an evening local passenger train, the 5.40 pm, leaves for Cambridge and home behind E4 Class 2-4-0 No 62796, with its two ex. Great Eastern Railway carriages. The writing was on the wall for No 62796 with withdrawal occurring in May 1957 from 31A Cambridge. (Peter Hay)

22) Having taken on fresh coal supplies at the antiquated, smoke-stained and soot-encrusted coal stage at 36A Doncaster, Thompson A2/3 Class 4-6-2 No 60514 *Chamossaire,* from 34E New England and equipped with a rimless chimney, waits patiently for its next move in October 1958. Constructed in 1946, *Chamossaire* spent much of its working life operating from New England, being taken out of service from there in December 1962. (Stuart Pitchforth)

23)   Steam finale in East Anglia. B1 Class 4-6-0 No 61300, renumbered as Departmental locomotive No 23 and sister engine No
        61233 (Departmental No 21) in steam together at 31A Cambridge on 11th December 1964 during the demolition of the shed
        buildings. Both engines had been based at 31B March prior to becoming Departmental stock. No 61233 was finally withdrawn
        in April 1966 and No 61300 in November 1965. (H.L. Holland)

24)   The main lines and yards at Hornsey as taken from a different angle to that in picture number seven. A bunker-first Gresley
        N2 Class 0-6-2T No 69579, from 34A Kings Cross, eases a lengthy empty coaching stock train, including some sleeper cars,
        out of the carriage sidings on 6th June 1959 and heads for Kings Cross. In July 1960 No 69579 was transferred to the near
        at hand Hornsey shed, coded 34B. (F. Hornby)

25)   A light and airy atmosphere inside the roundhouse at 31F Spital Bridge (Peterborough) in 1958. From left to right, all out of steam, are three locally based engines — B1 Class 4-6-0 No 61095, Riddles WD Class 8F 2-8-0 No 90063 (with a NOT TO BE MOVED sign on the bufferbeam) and LMS Class 3F 'Jinty' 0-6-0T No 47300. All three engines moved on to pastures new, prior to or when the shed closed in February 1960. (A.C. Ingram)

26)   Two gaunt chimneys dominate the skyline at 41E Staveley (Barrow Hill) on 25th July 1965, where there is a mixed bag of steam power on show in the shed yard. In the background is a line of LMS Ivatt Class 4 'Flying Pig' 2-6-0's. In front of them is an LMS Class 8F 2-8-0 which is backing on to another 'Flying Pig' No 43089, a Barrow Hill engine, and a WD Class 8F 2-8-0. Barrow Hill became Eastern Region property in February 1958. (E.L. Rivett)

27) A maze of lines meet and criss-cross over one another at Spalding on 2nd August 1963. B1 Class 4-6-0 No 61302, allocated to 34E New England, cautiously negotiates pointwork and trundles over a level crossing and passes a signalbox, its progress being observed by a lone pedestrian, with a lengthy freight consisting in the main of empty flat wagons. (T.R. Amos)

28) Looking south at Cambridge on 2nd April 1956 we see former GER E4 Class 2-4-0 No 62796 bringing some empty stock from the sidings towards the north end of the long platform, which will be gained by using the scissors crossing behind the camera. Trains standing head to head or back to back, at the same platform, were a common local sight. The interesting signals in the foreground help to complete this picture. (Peter Hay)

29)	The driver of especially spruced up (complete with a white painted cab roof) D16/3 Class 4-4-0 No 62605, from 31B March, takes a well earned smoke-break at Hitchin on 30th April 1956 after bringing in a Stephenson Locomotive Society special into the station from Kings Cross via the Hertford Loop. This 'Claud Hamilton' had been built in 1911, rebuilt in March 1940 and was taken out of traffic in June 1957 from March. (F. Hornby)

30)	One of the initial members of the Thompson B1 Class 4-6-0's No 61003 *Gazelle,* allocated to 30F Parkeston (Harwich), has steam lifting gently from its safety valves on 10th August 1957, whilst standing light engine at Liverpool Street station. *Gazelle* remained at various depots in the Great Eastern Division until November 1959 when it was drafted to the Great Northern section at 36A Doncaster. (N.L. Browne)

31)   A quartet of condensing apparatus equipped Gresley N2 Class 0-6-2 Tanks on a weed overgrown road at 34C Hatfield in June 1957. Two of the quartet can be identified as Nos 69498, from 34A Kings Cross and No 69502, from 34B Hornsey. The fact that all four are out of steam possibly points to this being a Sunday. Hatfield shed, one of the more nondescript places, closed its doors to steam in January 1961. (Ken Ellis)

32)   Yet another photograph of a B1 Class 4-6-0. A stiff winter breeze blows smoke and steam from the tall chimney on the station building and from No 61313, a 41D Canklow locomotive, at Sheffield (Midland) on 7th February 1964, the skyline being dominated by mammoth blocks of flats. No doubt the two enginemen in front of the cab of No 61313 will be glad to climb aboard and share the warmth from the firebox. (B.J. Ashworth)

33) One mile after starting from Cambridge, D16/3 'Claud Hamilton' Class 4-4-0 No 62530 (31A Cambridge) and an unidentified B1 Class 4-6-0 burst out from Coldham Lane bridge, bound for Ely. Rather than a heavy express requiring double heading, this is a local stopping service, as the white headcode disc proclaims. Nevertheless the pair make a brave sight on 2nd April 1956. (Peter Hay)

34) Like all the other regions which make up British Railways the Great Eastern section has its own crack trains which carry famous headboards. A somewhat underpowered *The Day Continental* stands in a platform at Harwich Parkeston Quay West station behind K3 Class 2-6-0 No 61942, from 30A Stratford, with the fireman passing the time of day with his driver on Sunday 27th June 1954. (J.H. Price)

35) A mechanical hoist in use in the background of this photograph is probably loading ash into the wagons behind Gresley 02/2 Class 2-8-0 No 63940, a very clean visitor to 31B March from 35B Grantham in September 1956. No 63940 remained at Grantham until it was subjected to a 'theoretical' transfer to 36A Doncaster in September 1963, the very same month it was condemned. (L. Brownhill)

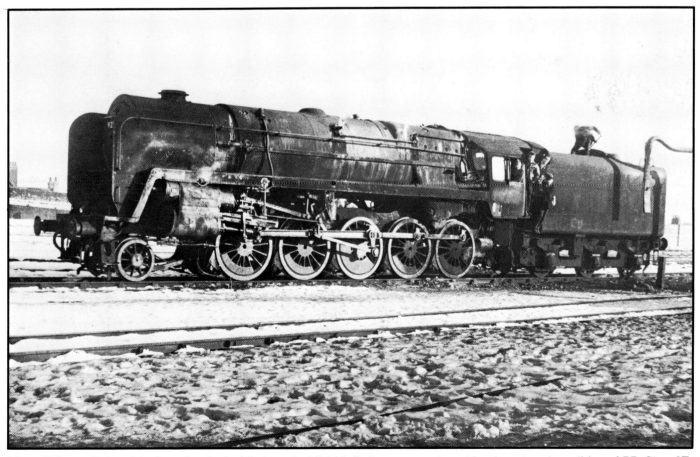

36) What a disgraceful advert for the 'public image' of British Railways as portrayed by the external condition of BR Class 9F 2-10-0 No 92149, from 34E New England in January 1962. The location is the snow covered shed yard at 34B Hornsey where No 92149 is being prepared for its return freight working from Ferme Park to New England. Four Hornsey cleaners look towards the camera from the footplate. (P. Cane)

37) A view inside part of the interior of the gloomy Eastern Region owned roundhouse at 41D Canklow on Sunday, 14th February 1965. Stabled adjacent to an unoccupied road is LMS Class 4 'Flying Pig' 2-6-0 No 43091 (with a chalked 41D shedcode on the smokebox). Accompanying No 43091 is another Canklow inmate WD Class 8F 2-8-0 No 90471, with an unidentified sister engine in the extreme right of the picture. (M.S. Stokes)

38) An all but deserted scene at the smoke-blackened Kings Cross terminus in 1959 where just one human being can be noted on one of the platforms, in the shape of a 'spotter' who is looking in the opposite direction to where we espy a less than clean B1 Class 4-6-0 No 61317, a 32A Norwich engine, which is departing with an express for Cambridge. A move in February 1960 took No 61317 to a different home at 40A Lincoln. (R.W. Hinton)

39)   A large number of passengers await their transport within the darkness of the canopy covered right hand platform at Peterborough (East) on 28th March 1959. The station's island platform is littered with unemployed trolleys as LMS Class 4F 0-6-0 No 44463, from 21A Saltley, passes a diesel multiple unit, which is on a shuttle service to Peterborough (North), on a freight working. (F. Hornby)

40)   A gasholder looks down upon J6 Class 0-6-0 No 64244, of 40F Boston, which, with safety valves roaring, departs from Boston station in bright sunshine in charge of a short 'express' (excursion) to Skegness on Whit Sunday, 29th June 1953. No 64244 was to remain faithful to Boston shed until no longer required by the Motive Power authorities in June 1958. Scrapping came at Doncaster Works the following month. (L. Perrin)

41) Still carrying its number 13 from the Edward Thompson reign and also the raised letters L.N.E.R. on the tender, A4 Class 4-6-2 60013 *Dominion of New Zealand* lies dead in the shed yard at Doncaster on 3rd April 1949. Keeping *Dominion of Canada* company are V2 Class 2-6-2 No 60803 and J6 Class 0-6-0 No 64212. At this stage in time British Railways was in its infancy and it was years before there was standard uniformity of loco numbers. (A.N.H. Glover)

42) A freight train of empty flat wagons trail along behind Riddles War Department Class 8F 2-8-0 No 90131, from 40B Immingham, as it heads northbound at Firsby on 4th June 1963. Three months later No 90131 was transferred to 36E Retford, its final home, being condemned in March 1965. Firsby station, between Boston and Louth, fared little better, being closed down in 1970. (J. Schatz)

43)   With Christmas fast approaching an unkempt BR *Britannia* Class 4-6-2 No 70041 *Sir John Moore,* allocated to 32A Norwich, momentarily disturbs the overhead wires at Stratford with its exhaust, as it hurries out of London with a down relief express on 23rd December 1959. *Sir John Moore* was drafted away from Norwich shed to 40B Immingham in December 1960. (B.W.L. Brooksbank)

44)   A grubby water column stands guard over a bedraggled former London Tilbury & Southend locomotive in the shape of Class 3 4-4-2T No 41977, from 33A Plaistow, which is a visitor to 33C Shoeburyness on 13th April 1958. The bulk of the surviving members of this class were withdrawn en masse in February 1959, including No 41977. Stored at Winsford on the LMR from February 1959 they were despatched for scrapping in early 1960. (A.N.H. Glover)

45) With a plume of white smoke cascading from the tall chimney, a Great Eastern Railway, Worsdell inspired — Holden rebuilt J15 Class 0-6-0 No 65453, allocated to 30F Parkeston, is photographed on a freight near to Manningtree in April 1956. The short Great Eastern section goods — trucks and a tank wagon, are well within the capabilities of No 65453. (Peter Hay)

46) The name of Frodingham (Scunthorpe) is associated with the steel producing industry, now very much scaled down compared to many years ago. To cope with the rail traffic Frodingham has its own shed, coded 36C, to house its own inmates and visiting locomotives. With a Robinson Great Central 04 Class 2-8-0 in attendance a Frodingham based WD Class 8F 2-8-0 No 90031 rattles a steel train past the camera in September 1961. (G.W. Sharpe)

47)   The unique A1/1 Class 4-6-2 No 60113 *Great Northern* in the yard of its home depot at 35B Grantham, in steam on 3rd October 1954. *Great Northern* is a 1945 Thompson rebuild of Gresley's 1922 built A10 Class Pacific No 4470. Another feature which differed from all of the other A1's is the different style of smoke deflectors. In the latter years of its working life it was based at 36A Doncaster being withdrawn in December 1962. (R. Butterfield)

48)   A peaceful scene at Essendine on the East Coast Main Line is disturbed by the activities of WD Class 8F 2-8-0 No 90063, of 36A Doncaster, as it shunts a brake van onto the rear of an up freight train in the sidings adjacent to the main running lines prior to running round and heading for the south on 5th September 1963. No 90063 remained at Doncaster shed until the end of steam on the Eastern Region in April 1966. (K.L. Seal)

49)	The last Great Northern Railway 0-6-0 goods design had a superheater and piston valves which produced a very useful engine with, if necessary, mixed traffic abilities. Some of those shedded at 35A New England (Peterborough) were sub-shedded at Spalding and like No 64220, seen on 4th April 1956, were fitted with a tablet exchanger for use on the former Midland & Great Northern Joint lines. (Peter Hay)

50)	A line-up of grubby workhorses outside 40B Immingham shed on 28th April 1963. On view from left to right are — an unidentified WD Class 8F 2-8-0, 02/3 Class 2-8-0 No 63980, from 36E Retford, WD Class 8F 2-8-0 No 90460, another visitor, this one from 40A Lincoln and a home based, double chimney equipped BR Class 9F 2-10-0 No 92197. Immingham shed, which once housed a massive allocation of steam closed to the same in February 1966. (F. Hornby)

51) A photographer straddles a single section of point rodding between the Midland and Great Northern main lines as it passes Wisbech West Junction signalbox (Midland Railway) at Peterborough after he has recorded his photograph of a filthy, smokebox scorched, A3 Class 4-6-2 No 60076 *Galopin* (52A Gateshead) with an up Kings Cross bound express in 1958. The line to Wisbech is via the overbridge behind the signalbox. (A.C. Ingram)

52) 04/2 Class 2-8-0 No 63680, from 41A Sheffield (Darnall), is just about to pass under the smoke-grimed gloom of the overall roof at Sheffield (Victoria), running tender-first with a train of empty wooden coal wagons. The one coupled to the engine on 27th August 1951 still retains the old grease-filled axleboxes. (Peter Hay)

53)   Locomotives of London Midland & Scottish and the Midland Railway combine to double-head a local passenger train at Peterborough. Fowler Class 4F 0-6-0 No 44184, from 15C Leicester (Midland), pilots Class 2P 4-4-0 No 40543, a Fowler rebuild of a Johnson design and also from Leicester (Midland), as they restart a Peterborough (East) to Leicester service in 1958. (A.C. Ingram)

54)   Passengers in the leading coach of this lightly loaded Ongar to Epping local train will be pleased that the wind is carrying away the smoke issuing from F5 Class 2-4-2T No 67193, based at 30A Stratford, as they leave North Weald on 1st April 1956. Maybe the fire is getting low on No 67193. It was condemned in November 1957 whilst still allocated to Stratford. (Peter Hay)

55)   Overbridges of different designs dominate the northern end of the station at Sandy, on the East Coast Main Line in the Spring of 1958. A3 Class 4-6-2 No 60048 *Doncaster,* rather ironically allocated to its namesake shed of 36A, steams under one of the bridges and heads for Kings Cross with an up express. The shedplate has lost one of its holding bolts and is hanging down at an angle on the smokebox door. (A.C. Ingram)

56)   40E Colwick, a massive steam shed installation on the outskirts of Nottingham, is visited by the photographer on 18th November 1962. The focus of attention is LMS Class 4 'Flying Pig' 2-6-0 No 43104, a visitor from 40A Lincoln. Behind No 43104 is a member of the WD Class 8F 2-8-0's and an L1 Class 2-6-4T. Next to No 43104 is yet another WD Class 8F 2-8-0 of which there are many allocated to Colwick. (J. Schatz)

57) A member of the footplate crew peers out of the cab of his charge, 36A Doncaster based A1 Class 4-6-2 No 60139 *Sea Eagle,* seen here light engine in March 1963 at Doncaster station. *Sea Eagle* is possibly on station pilot or main line standby duty at this stage in time. It was constructed under British Railways ownership in 1948 and only had a working life of sixteen years, being condemned in June 1964. (N.E. Preedy)

58) As well as pre-grouping rolling stock, the railway scene in the 1950's contained many other relics of the days before 1923, like the ex. Great Eastern Railway signal at Whitlingham, the first station out of Norwich, which closed in 1955. Coming past with a goods train on 5th April 1956 is J17 Class 0-6-0 No 65566, very much a local engine from 32A Norwich shed. It was withdrawn from the same in July 1960. (Peter Hay)

59) An almost pure Great Central setting at 41J Langwith Junction on 27th June 1963. In view in the GC shed yard are two home-sprung Robinson 2-8-0's, from the O4/8 Class Nos 63731 and 63800. The usurper is a WD Class 2-8-0. The depot consists of two narrow running sheds and a cramped yard. Upon closure on 6th February 1966 its former tasks were taken over by a diesel depot at Shirebrook. (N.E. Preedy)

60) Having disgorged themselves from their carriages, numbers of enthusiasts go on a walk-about at Beccles, between Ipswich and Lowestoft. The five coach train is a special organised by the Railway Enthusiasts Club — 'Suffolk Venturer' on 30th September 1952. In charge of the train is Worsdell/Holden J15 Class 0-6-0 No 65447 (32B Ipswich) which has stopped en route to the Waveney Valley line. (F. Hornby)

61) With just a slight wisp of steam emerging from the safety valve, former Deeley Midland Railway Class 0F 0-4-0T No 41533 takes a rest between duties at Staveley Iron Works on 5th March 1961. Note the small coal supply atop the firebox and the fact that No 41533 is still sporting the old style 'lion & wheel' logo despite looking apparently ex. works. This loco has been supplied to Staveley Works from the near at hand shed 41E Staveley (Barrow Hill). (A.N.H. Glover)

62) The 'Crimpsall' erecting bay at Doncaster Works hosts two Pacific engines on an unknown date in the 1950's. In various stages of overhaul are A3 Class 4-6-2 No 60089 *Felstead*, from 64B Haymarket and A2 Class 4-6-2 No 60538 *Velocity* (fitted with a double blastpipe and chimney), of 52A Gateshead. The latter was constructed in 1948 whereas the former was built twenty years earlier. (Stuart Pitchforth)

63)   A view of 34A Kings Cross shed just one month before closure, taken on 18th May 1963. Lined up in front of the depot from left to right are — V2 Class 2-6-2 No 60803 (34E New England), A1 Class 4-6-2 No 60148 *Aboyeur* (56C Copley Hill), V2 Class 2-6-2 No 60941 (50A York), A1 Class 4-6-2 No 60119 *Patrick Stirling* (36A Doncaster) and A4 Class 4-6-2 60034 *Lord Faringdon,* the latter being a Kings Cross inmate. (Peter Hay)

64)   The 10.15 am Cambridge to Kings Lynn arriving at March on 3rd April 1956. D16 Class 4-4-0 No 62562 (31B March) is nicely cleaned with its splasher beading polished, perhaps because this is the return working of the engine off the up *Fenman* which left Wisbech at 7.30 am. The named train's headboard is carried reversed above the bufferbeam, but the headcode disc position shows this is a stopping train. (Peter Hay)

65) Grantham station is swathed in bright sunshine in the early Spring of 1958. A3 Class 4-6-2 No 60091 *Captain Cuttle*, from 52B Heaton, enters the station with a Newcastle to Kings Cross express. Later equipped with a double chimney and German smoke deflectors, *Captain Cuttle* was shunted between 51A Darlington, 52A Gateshead and 52B Heaton sheds before being withdrawn from service in October 1964. (Stuart Pitchforth)

66) Engine and brake on duty at Langwith Junction in September 1965. An uncared for Riddles Class 8F 2-8-0 No 90149, based at the near at hand 41J shed ekes out the remainder of its working life with condemnation only a few short months away in January 1966. No 90149 had spent much of its life at various depots on the Western Region before being transferred to the Eastern Region at 41F Mexborough in December 1962. (G.W. Sharpe)

67) We end our sojourn onto the Eastern Region with two photographs taken on the Great Eastern section. The first is a general view of Hackney Downs Junction station on 20th September 1958 with its lofty signalbox, cross-overs and speed restrictions. Approaching the station from the Enfield direction is a five coach local passenger bound for Liverpool Street hauled by an unidentified N7 Class 0-6-2T. (F. Hornby)

68) The second print is a panoramic view of the main lines, freight and passenger sidings and shed (31A) at Cambridge in 1957. Note the variety of upper and lower quadrant signals scattered round the vicinity. In the centre of the frame are a number of different types of steam motive power including a K3 Class 2-6-0. The shed closed its doors to steam on 18th June 1962. (R.S. Carpenter)

69) There were a mass of avoiding lines carrying freight traffic in and around the vicinity of York station in steam days. Former North Eastern Railway J27 Class 0-6-0 No 65844 struggles for adhesion whilst hauling a northbound transfer freight on the loop at the southern end of the station on 1st September 1964. No 65844 had been the property of 50A York shed since a transfer from 50F Malton in April 1963 after the latter had closed. (M.S. Stokes)

70) Once part of the proud trio of BR *Britannia* Class 4-6-2's based on the Southern Region, No 70009 *Alfred the Great,* from 12A Carlisle (Kingmoor) and stripped of nameplates, finds itself on a more mundane duty than it was designed for in the twilight of its career in the summer of 1966. *Alfred the Great* waits to depart from Wellington Street Goods depot, Leeds (City) station. It was withdrawn in January 1967. (Stuart Pitchforth)

71) Smoke, signals and shadow at Wakefield. A wintry sun highlights the exhaust being hurled skywards by an unidentified Riddles Austerity War Department Class 8F 2-8-0 as it hauls a seemingly endless rake of coal wagons round the south west of the triangle at Wakefield (Lancashire & Yorkshire) and heads for the station on 6th March 1965. Today it is rare to even see these types of wagons let alone such a lengthy freight train. (H.L. Holland)

72) A Sunday gathering of former North Eastern Railway J27 Class 0-6-0's at 51B Newport (Tees-side) on 12th August 1956. Nos 65766 (left) and 65745 are shedded here and display the two varieties of chimney and cab spectacle glass seen on this class. WD Class 8F 2-8-0 No 90074, again a local engine, represents a short-lived modernisation of freight power in the area. (Peter Hay)

73) Another view of York station (beneath the girder bridge) from a platform at Holgate (racecourse). A Manchester based (9D Newton Heath) LMS Class 5 4-6-0 No 45339 accelerates towards the south with a heavily loaded mineral train on 19th May 1964. The end of the freight is still on the goods lines, avoiding the passenger station. The six track section at Holgate is an ideal spotters vantage point. (H.L. Holland)

74)   A fine elevated view from Wakefield (Westgate) station, once of joint Great Central and Great Northern origin, looking southwards over the simple track and pointwork during the late 1950's. Standing in the station at this point in time is Thompson B1 Class 4-6-0 No 61170, from 36A Doncaster, in charge of a local passenger working. (Stuart Pitchforth)

75)   Selby, on the East Coast Main Line, is the setting for this fine portrait of one of Sir Nigel Gresley's masterpieces — A4 Class 4-6-2 No 60009 *Union of South Africa,* from 64B Haymarket, as it sweeps through with a non-stop working of the *Elizabethan* in 1960, the penultimate year for steam power on this crack express. Thirty plus years on and happily *Union of South Africa* is still with us in an active role. (Stuart Pitchforth)

76) Bright sunshine invades the small roundhouse at 51A Darlington, used to house tank engine types like J50 0-6-0 Tanks Nos 68898 and 68959 seen on 15th March 1959. Also present is J94 Class 0-6-0 Saddle Tank No 68015. All three are native to Darlington. No 68015 moved to 56B Ardsley in December 1960. No 68898 to 56A Wakefield in June 1959 with No 68959 following to the same two months later. (T.R. Amos)

77) If ever an engine shed had a favourite locomotive then it must be LMS *Jubilee* Class 4-6-0 No 45581 *Bihar and Orissa* for many years a longstanding inmate at 55C Farnley Junction. Here it is seen in steam towards the end of its career alongside its home shed in the early summer of 1966. Condemned in August of the same year *Bihar and Orissa* lay in store at Farnley until despatched to Drapers, Hull in November 1966. (Stuart Pitchforth)

78) In the shadow of the New Castle Gresley V3 Class 2-6-2T No 67684 (52A Gateshead) fusses around light engine during station pilot duties at Newcastle (Central) on 10th February 1964. Prior to being allocated to Gateshead No 67684 was based at a variety of sheds from the late 1950's onwards — 53B Hull (Botanic Gardens), 51D Middlesbrough and 53A/50B Hull (Dairycoates). It was withdrawn from Gateshead in November 1964. (B.J. Ashworth)

79) G5 Class 0-4-4T No 67341 (52F Blyth) is the motive power for a Blyth to Newsham and Monkseaton local train on 15th August 1956. With three bogies and a van it is seen here at the start of its journey as clouds of black exhaust enshroud the overhead signal gantry. Before condemnation in November 1958 No 67341 served from three more depots, 53B Hull (Botanic Gardens), 53D Bridlington and finally 53A Hull (Dairycoates). (Peter Hay)

80) Another view of Wakefield, this time looking basically north towards Westgate station with the motive power depot to be seen in the frame. A1 Class 4-6-2 No 60144 *King's Courier,* from 36A Doncaster, heads towards the camera with a diverted Sunday Leeds to Kings Cross express. It has been diverted through Kirkgate station, on L & Y tracks, before joining the G.N. main line at Hare Park Junction, south of Wakefield in 1961. (Stuart Pitchforth)

81) A York to Newcastle (Central) express via Hartlepool winds its way round the extreme curve at the latter location during a bright summer's day in 1960. In charge of this express is 52B Heaton based A2 Class 4-6-2 No 60539 *Bronzino.* This locomotive is the last member of the class to be constructed (1948) and also one of the first to be condemned, from 52D Tweedmouth in October 1962 after only fourteen years of life. (N.E. Preedy)

82) A dull winter's day at Morpeth (curve) sees Class J27 0-6-0 No 65855, of 52F Blyth, coming off the Bedlington/Blyth branch and passing Wansbeck signalbox with a mineral train on 10th February 1964. The original Blyth & Tyne station at Morpeth closed as early as 1880 whilst the two intermediate stations at Hepscott and Choppington on the Bedlington branch had demised in 1950. Bedlington closed to passengers in 1964. (B.J. Ashworth)

83) The LNER J77 Class 0-6-0 Tanks preserved a Victorian look into British Railways days by virtue of their exposed leading springs, tea-caddy sandboxes and the rounded cabs fitted by York Works when it rebuilt them from the much older 0-4-4 Tanks. The age and ancestry of the six wheeler in the shed yard at 51E Stockton is unknown, but it made No 68438, a local engine, look modern in comparison on 12th August 1956. (Peter Hay)

84) The protective tarpaulin sheet has been slung loosely onto the top of the cab of former North Eastern Railway J27 Class 0-6-0 No 65817, allocated to 52G Sunderland, as it trundles into West Hartlepool at the head of a pick-up freight in September 1965. For many years an inmate at Sunderland No 65817 had brief forays at 51L Thornaby and 52E Percy Main in 1964 before returning again to Sunderland in February 1965. (N.E. Preedy)

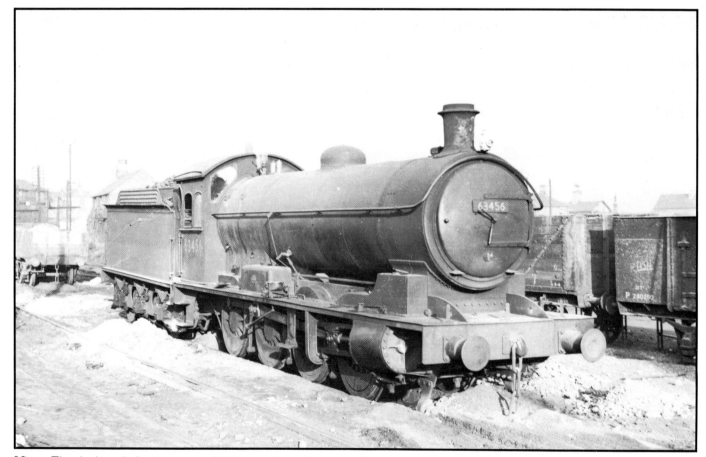

85) The shed tracks in the yard at 54C Borough Gardens has all but disappeared under a screen of discarded ash in April 1953. The main subject of the photographer is locally based ex. NER Class Q6 0-8-0 No 63456. Borough Gardens changed codes to 52J in September 1958, a code it only carried for a short period of time for the shed closed down in June 1959. Upon closure No 63456 moved on to 52C Blaydon. (N.E. Preedy)

86)   A2/3 Class 4-6-2 No 500 *Edward Thompson* was constructed in 1946, the 2,000th locomotive to be built at Doncaster and it was named after its designer. The A2/3's were the last Pacifics to be designed by him. It is seen here in the yard at York shed on 13th June 1949 with BRITISH RAILWAYS on the tender. It was later renumbered 60500 and had its rimless double chimney replaced with a more standard rimmed one. (A.N.H. Glover)

87)   A lengthy row of terraced houses, synonymous with the railway scene for many years, look down upon Darlington station on a hot August day in 1960, where there is a combination of ancient and modern on show. Carrying express headlamps one of the batch of British Railways built (1949-1951) J72 Class 0-6-0 Tanks No 69022 (51A Darlington) is in charge of the NER 'Inspector's Saloon' No 900272 (vintage unknown). (Ken Ellis)

88) A busy situation in and around the vicinity of Normanton station and freight yards during the 1960's. LMS Stanier Class 5 4-6-0 No 44852, a 55A Leeds (Holbeck) locomotive, passes the station at caution and heads south past Normanton Station North signalbox with a lengthy parcels train. To the right and behind No 44852 is an unidentified WD Class 8F 2-8-0 on a freight working at a stand at signals. (Stuart Pitchforth)

89) Another 1960's photograph, this time in the shed yard at 50B Hull (Dairycoates), with a close-up of a begrimed member of the B1 fleet of 4-6-0's based at the depot, No 61012 *Puku*. Allocated to Dairycoates from 52A Gateshead in August 1960, *Puku* remained at the shed until December 1966, six months before it closed to steam, being drafted to its final base at 50A York, being withdrawn from there in June 1967. (Stuart Pitchforth)

90)   A work-stained freight workhorse WD Class 8F 2-8-0 No 90445 simmers outside the straight, but narrow, three road running shed at its home base 51C West Hartlepool on 14th June 1966. From January 1957 onwards No 90445 had worked from 54B Tyne Dock, 50A York, 56A Wakefield and 51L Thornaby before being drafted to West Hartlepool in May 1964. It was withdrawn from the shed a month after this picture was taken. (N.E. Preedy)

91)   Two water columns guard the entrance to the canopy covered station at Bridlington in August 1962. At the head of a summer excursion is another named B1 Class 4-6-0 No 61013 *Topi,* from 56B Ardsley, which is parked adjacent to an intricately designed cast-iron elevated water tank. *Topi,* a longstanding favourite at Ardsley moved on to 56A Wakefield in October 1965 when the latter was closed. (Stuart Pitchforth)

92) 40B Immingham based BR *Britannia* Class 4-6-2 No 70036 *Boadicea*, with a clear road ahead, pauses for refreshment at Sowerby Bridge with an excursion during the summer of 1962. With the driver seated in the cab and no obvious sign of his fireman it is somewhat of a mystery as to who is going to prevent the water from overflowing out of the tender! (Stuart Pitchforth)

93) Weak winter sunshine filters into Leeds (Central) station in December 1961 and helps to highlight the arrival of A1 Class 4-6-2 No 60117 *Bois Roussel* at the end of its journey from Kings Cross with a down express. Soon after coming to a halt *Bois Roussel* will be detached and despatched to its home shed at 56C Copley Hill for servicing. When Copley Hill closed in September 1964 *Bois Roussel* was drafted to 56B Ardsley. (Kit Windle)

94) A very much under-photographed shed was at Consett, in County Durham, coded 54D by BR in 1949. Originally it only had one track, but this became two in 1950. In 1958 it was recoded 52K which it retained until closure in May 1965. The bulk of its allocation consisted of K1 Class 2-6-0's and Q6 Class 0-8-0's of which we can see a variety of the same on shed in July 1964, one K1 being No 62027. (R. Bartlett)

95) One of the fast disappearing North Eastern Region LMS *Jubilee* Class 4-6-0's No 45565 *Victoria*, from 56F Low Moor, is captured on film in August 1966 passing through Halifax with an express. Although still carrying number and shedplates the nameplates have been removed being replaced with chalked names — a poor substitute for the real thing. Another photographer has recorded his shot for posterity from the signalbox. (Stuart Pitchforth)

96) The North East, where steam railways were born, was one of the last areas in Britain where BR steam was still working in the late 1960's, and on coal traffic too, which was very appropriate. An added attraction was the presence of pre-Grouping engines in the shape of NER J27 Class 0-6-0's like No 65855, from 52F Blyth, here nearing Wardleys House Junction, near Bedlington in June 1966. (Peter Hay)

97) Passengers at former London North Eastern Railway stations in the north east were often favoured with well designed all-over roofs at the bigger stations like Darlington. On 31st August 1952 A8 Class 4-6-2T No 69862 is seen returning to its home base at Stockton with a local passenger service. Withdrawn from 54A Sunderland in July 1958 No 69862 was stored at Darlington Works for two months before being cut up there. (Peter Hay)

98)   The twin cooling towers are a give-away as to this location — 56A Wakefield, where we find two steam stalwarts which have reached the end of the line. Stripped of coupling rods WD Class 8F 2-8-0 No 90470 and BR Class 9F 2-10-0 No 92001 await their last call to the breakers yard in January 1967. No 90470 went to Drapers, Hull and No 92001 to Cox and Danks, Wadsley Bridge later in 1967. (Stuart Pitchforth)

99)   In welcome contrast to the above picture we return once again to the subject of 'live' steam, this time in the yard at 52A Gateshead in 1960. Locally based A4 Class 4-6-2 No 60001 *Sir Ronald Matthews,* with what appears to be a slightly distorted nameplate, simmers over the ash disposal pits. Despite the ever increasing ranks of main line diesels, *Sir Ronald Matthews* survived in service at Gateshead until October 1964. (Stuart Pitchforth)

100) The driver looks forward proudly from his charge, the world record holder for steam, A4 Class 4-6-2 No 60022 *Mallard* (34A Kings Cross), in pristine condition, as it sweeps majestically round the 45 mph restricted curve immediately to the north of York station with the down non-stop *Elizabethan,* from Kings Cross to Edinburgh (Waverley) — circa 1960. In the background, under repair, is York Minster. (Stuart Pitchforth)

101) A gloomy day in 1961 is brightened up by the presence of highly polished BR Class 4 2-6-4T No 80116, from 55H Leeds (Neville Hill). No 80116 is proudly carrying the train headboard of the *Yorkshire Pullman* at Bradford (Exchange) prior to taking the express forward to Leeds. Transferred to Neville Hill in May 1958, from 50G Whitby, No 80116 ultimately ended up on the Scottish Region being withdrawn in May 1967. (Stuart Pitchforth)

102) When one thinks of depots like 56C Copley Hill one immediately conjures up pictures of the mighty A3 and A1 Classes of Pacifics utilised on the express services to and from Leeds. It of course had classes of less distinct pedigrees such as J6 Class 0-6-0 No 64277 seen in the shed yard in company with an unknown K3 Class 2-6-0 on 27th August 1961. A sister engine to No 64277 is in the right of the frame. (T.R. Amos)

103) A fine view of Wakefield (Kirkgate) during 1960. In the centre LMS Class 4 2-6-4T No 42650, from 56A Wakefield, makes ready to depart with a three coach local passenger train. To the right of No 42650, light engine, is ex. works LMS Hughes Class 6P5F 'Crab' 2-6-0 No 42846, a 'stranger in the camp' from far off 21A Saltley, in Birmingham. Kirkgate station was once the joint property of the GN and L & Y. (Stuart Pitchforth)

104) Old goods engines like former North Eastern Railway J25 Class 0-6-0 No 65683, from a design first introduced in 1898, were still thought worthy of a full overhaul and repaint in 1952, and so it stands outside Darlington Works on 31st August, ready to leave for its home shed at nearby 51F West Auckland. It had another six years of work to give to its owners, being withdrawn in June 1958 from 50A York. (Peter Hay)

105) One of the fleet of 64B Haymarket based A4 Class 4-6-2's No 60011 *Empire of India* steams through Heaton, the second station northbound from Newcastle with the *Queen of Scots* (Kings Cross-Leeds-Harrogate-Newcastle-Edinburgh (Waverley)-Glasgow (Queen Street) express in the early spring of 1960. *Empire of India* remained at Haymarket until ousted by diesel power in June 1962, moving on to 61B Aberdeeen (Ferryhill). (Stuart Pitchforth)

106) An overcast and misty day at Leeds (Central) witnesses the departure of Copley Hill based A1 Class 4-6-2 No 60141 *Abbotsford* with a Pullman express from the vantage point of stairs belonging to the signalbox on the right. Photographed circa 1955/56 strictly speaking this is an Eastern Region photo, but as a transfer to the North Eastern was imminent it was decided to include it in the latter chapter. (Stuart Pitchforth)

107) A quartet of ex. North Eastern Railway Q6 Class 0-8-0's are lined up in the shed yard at 51L Thornaby on 15th March 1959, some nine months after the depot was commissioned. Three can be identified as Nos 63396, 63388 and 63375, all Thornaby engines. All three were part of the initial allocation of locos to Thornaby in June 1958, No 63375 from 51D Middlesbrough and Nos 63388 and 63396 from 51B Newport. (T.R. Amos)

108) With the regulator wide open, the exhaust is thrown high into the winter sky from the funnel of Gresley J50/3 Class 0-6-0T No 68948, from 56B Ardsley, as it struggles to move a lengthy transfer freight along near Wakefield on 14th January 1957. Between May 1958 and October 1959 No 68948 was subjected to a spate of transfers to 51D Middlesbrough, 51L Thornaby, 50C Selby, 56C Copley Hill and 56F Low Moor. (D.K. Jones)

109) The two centre tracks in this picture taken on 28th August 1952 of Selby are the East Coast Main Line (now diverted round the town) and its notorious swingbridge bottleneck. The station sign is in the North Eastern Region colours of tangerine and white as ex. NER J27 Class 0-6-0 No 65857, from the local shed 50C, runs light engine through the down platform. (Peter Hay)

110) Alston, the terminus of the branch from Haltwhistle on the Carlisle-Newcastle line on 13th June 1956. BR Class 4 2-6-0 No 76024 (52C Blaydon) stands tender-first in the station with a Haltwhistle local passenger. The loco shed on the right is a sub-shed of Blaydon. The branch to Alston along with the associated stations at Featherstone Park, Coanwood, Lambley and Slaggyford closed during 1976. (F. Hornby)

111) The former Midland Railway motive power depot at 55A Leeds (Holbeck) although having been absorbed into the North Eastern Region in 1956/57 maintained the tradition of keeping former LMR power on its books, for the most part, right up to closure to steam on 1st October 1967. One of its fleet of LMS Class 5 4-6-0's No 44854 is photographed in the shed yard in steam on 9th June 1965. (T.R. Amos)

112) Raven designed former North Eastern Railway Q6 Class 0-8-0 No 63423, from 52G Sunderland, adds to the grime of the smoke-blackened wall at Gateshead as it clanks and wheezes tender-first past the camera heading eastbound with a mineral train on 10th February 1964. No 63423 is in its last year of revenue earning service being condemned from Sunderland in November. Darlington claimed the remains. (B.J. Ashworth)

113) The heavy snow which covered East Yorkshire in the winter of 1954/55 had melted by 20th March 1955, but nevertheless ex. NER J25 Class 0-6-0 No 65647, complete with snowplough, standing in the yard of its home shed at 50G Whitby, is prepared for any surprises which the weather might bring. At this date in time Whitby's allocation was almost exclusively engines from the former North Eastern Railway. (Peter Hay)

114) A section of the roundhouse at 52F North Blyth reveals three of the ex. NER J27 Class 0-6-0's on North Blyth's books Nos 65869, 65804 and 65801 (from left to right), the first two being devoid of shedplates on 30th May 1966. No 65801 was condemned two months later, but the other two were destined to live on into 1967, No 65869 at 52G Sunderland until February of that year and No 65804 at the same depot in July. (M. Rutter)

115) With repairs being attended to by a mobile crane from a bridge next to the station, a begrimed A1 Class 4-6-2 No 60146 *Peregrine*, from 50A York, has steam to spare as it departs from Sunderland with an express on 30th January 1962. *Peregrine* spent a few brief months at 55H Leeds (Neville Hill) between July and October 1963 before returning to York, a shed it was going to die at in October 1965. (D.K. Jones)

116)   The flashlight off the camera lights up the scene inside Darlington (Bank Top) station, with its overall roof curving away to the left. The flash also reflects the plume of excess steam issuing from the safety valves of V2 Class 2-6-2 No 60847, from 50A York, and fitted with outside steampipes as it stands light engine in a siding on 12th February 1964. Two small signals guard the two exit roads seen here. (B.J. Ashworth)

117)   With total closure on the immediate horizon all pretence at keeping one of its last surviving WD Class 8F 2-8-0's No 90405 clean has gone out of the window, that is assuming that 55E Normanton still had any locomotive cleaners left. No 90405 is seen in steam in the shed yard at Normanton in August 1967 taking fresh coal supplies prior to taking on one of its last duties before the depot demised the next month. (Stuart Pitchforth)

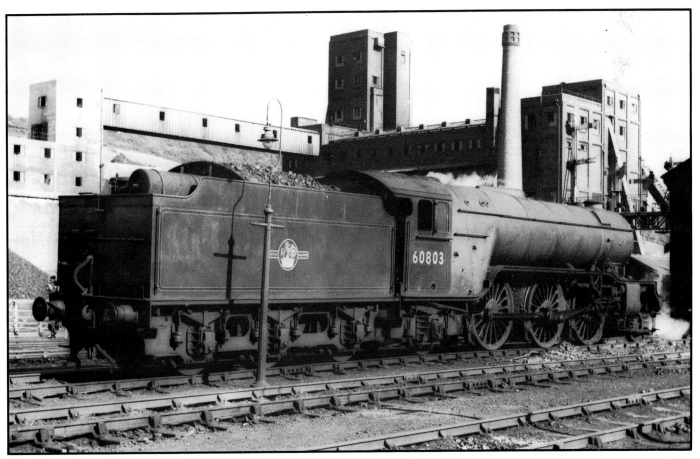

118) A typical steam shed scene with a near at hand industrial complex in the background. The scene is the shed yard at 50E Scarborough in the summer of 1961. The main subject of the photograph is 31B March allocated V2 Class 2-6-2 No 60803 which has worked to Scarborough on a special. The gas lit lamp and assortment of lower quadrant signals help to complete this picture. (Stuart Pitchforth)

119) Wet and overcast weather helps to accentuate the drifting steam from A5 Class 4-6-2T No 69840, a 51A Darlington locomotive, as it waits patiently to leave the terminus at Saltburn with a local passenger train bound for Darlington (Bank Top) on 11th August 1956. Note that no headcode lamp is fitted as yet. No 69840 demised at Darlington shed in September 1958. (Peter Hay)

120) A snow-laden sky threatens to cover the landscape at Tyne Dock on 10th February 1964, where there are a maze of tracks at different angles and curves to be seen. The lowering of a small signal enables ex. NER Q6 Class 0-8-0 No 63358, an inhabitant of 52H Tyne Dock shed, to slowly wheel its mineral cargo over pointwork in the right of the picture. No 63358 is just one month off condemnation. (B.J. Ashworth)

121) Another former Midland Railway shed which was absorbed into the North Eastern Region system in 1956/57 is Stourton which altered its 20B shedcode to 55B during the changeover of power. Again, like so many depots of its ilk, it retained former LMR power on its books as its mainstay. One of its allocation of LMS Class 8F 2-8-0's No 48274 is noted in a filthy condition in the yard at Stourton on 1st May 1966. (R. Turner)

122) The largest steam shed on the North Eastern Region was at Hull (Dairycoates), coded 53A by British Railways in 1949. At its height it had six turntables within a huge roundhouse and a straight running shed as well. Its code changed to 50B in January 1960 and here we see one of its vast allocation of WD Class 8F 2-8-0's No 90272 parked in what had become one of the exposed turntables on 20th August 1963. (B. Rands)

123) A3 Class 4-6-2 No 60051 *Blink Bonny*, newly transferred to 52B Heaton from 52A Gateshead, pauses briefly in West Hartlepool station in September 1962 at the head of a Newcastle to York train, a parcels, as the lamps on the bufferbeam indicate. Constructed during 1924 *Blink Bonny* had received a double chimney in August 1959 with the fitting of German smoke deflectors following on in March 1962. (N.E. Preedy)

124) Flat countryside at Crofton, near Wakefield, is the setting for this Sunday diversion in the summer of 1960. 34A Kings Cross 4-6-2 No 60025 *Falcon* glides towards the camera with what appears to be a Kings Cross to Leeds express having passed the signalbox at Crofton East Junction. Crofton itself once boasted passenger facilities, but had been closed since 1931. (Stuart Pitchforth)

125) The splendid arrays of elevated signals in the foreground and background almost disappear from sight being enveloped with the black exhaust emitting from the funnel of Raven inspired B16/1 Class 4-6-0 No 61415, an inhabitant of 50B Leeds (Neville Hill) as it heads an express at Scarborough during the 1950's with a rake of elderly stock. Condemned from Neville Hill in September 1961 it was not cut up until March 1963. (Stuart Pitchforth)

126) As a finale to the North Eastern chapter we take our leave with two fine shots of two locomotive sheds. The first is a ground view of 55D Royston during 1963. On view are several LMS Class 8F 2-8-0's and WD Class 8F 2-8-0's including Nos 48670 and 90488. Also in the frame is LMS Hughes Class 6P5F 'Crab' 2-6-0 No 42762, all Royston engines. Note the still hot ashes in the foreground. (Stuart Pitchforth)

127) The photographer must have had a head for heights for this elevated view of 56F Low Moor shed (Bradford) and station as taken from the coaling plant. At least two score locomotives can be seen mostly of LMS varieties including a 'Crab', Black 5's and Stanier 8F's — circa 1961. The first shed road on the left has a Thompson B1 4-6-0 on show. Low Moor shed eventually closed its doors forever in October 1967. (Stuart Pitchforth)

CHAPTER THREE — SCOTTISH REGION

128) Smartly maintained Gresley J38 Class 0-6-0 No 65924 is at peace with the world whilst simmering in the yard of its home shed at 62C Dunfermline adjacent to the small mechanical coaler in 1959. Dunfermline shed, of North British Railway origin, was situated to the south of the line east of Dunfermline (Upper) station (closed in 1968). No 65924 was withdrawn from the shed in June 1964 some three years before the depot closed. (Mike Higson)

129)   Monessie Gorge on the West Highland line as photographed from one of the rear carriages of an express on 23rd July 1956. Up front, two 65A Eastfield (Glasgow) LMS Class 5 4-6-0's Nos 44908 and 44956 combine to power the train on its arduous journey. No 44908 departed briefly from 65A in October 1957 to 67D Ardrossan, but returned again in January 1958. Both departed for ever from the shed by December 1962. (R. Butterfield)

130)   A pure North British setting at 64E Polmont on 6th September 1959 with J37 Class 0-6-0 No 64636 in attendance in front of the four road shed which has been home to this locomotive for many years. They eventually parted company on 17th May 1964, the day the shed died, with No 64636 moving the short distance to a new haven at 65F Grangemouth. It was only a short reprieve for it was withdrawn five months later. (A. Swain)

131) A lattice-work wrought iron bridge supported by cast-iron columns straddles the station at Newport-on-Tay East to enable travellers to cross the lines on 28th August 1963. Working tender-first on Tayport line duty is Thompson B1 Class 4-6-0 No 61180, from 62B Dundee Tay Bridge, about to depart and enter a single line section with the 6.40 pm passenger train from Tayport to Dundee. (A.F. Nisbet)

132) Once the pride of 52A Gateshead, A4 Class 4-6-2 No 60016 *Silver King* found itself wanted by the Scottish Region authorities to boost the steam passenger engine power on the enhanced Aberdeen to Glasgow services, being posted to 61B Aberdeen (Ferryhill) in November 1963. Here it is seen on the turntable at its home shed on 16th May 1964, with steam issuing from its cylinder cocks after servicing in readiness for its next duty. (T.R. Amos)

133) Without doubt, one of the finest stations in Scotland is Edinburgh (Waverley), deep in the heart of this great city, with the famous castle, gardens and Princes Street close at hand. A spruced up B1 Class 4-6-0 No 61324, of 64A St. Margarets (Edinburgh), departs from the south end of the station and heads for Carlton tunnel with a Stephenson Locomotive Society special on 14th April 1963. (J. Schatz)

134) A trio of railwaymen look proudly towards the camera from various vantage points on brand new British Railways built K1 Class 2-6-0 No 62003 in the shed yard at 65A Eastfield (Glasgow) on 19th June 1949. It is not known how long No 62003 remained in Scotland, but records show that by January 1957 it was on the North Eastern Region based at 51A Darlington. It was withdrawn in June 1965 after just sixteen years of life. (W. Boyden)

135) Before diesels arrived, double-headed LMS Class 5 4-6-0's were a common sight on expresses on the West Highland line. Two begrimed Black 5's Nos 44977, from 63B Fort William and 44707, of 65A Eastfield (Glasgow) are photographed at Bridge of Orchy, between Rannoch and Tyndrum, with a southbound Fort William to Glasgow (Queen Street) express on 18th June 1960. (F. Hornby)

136) The final member of the British Railways *Clan* Class 4-6-2's No 72009 *Clan Stewart,* a 68A Carlisle (Kingmoor) engine, steams along at Stonehaven with an up southbound T.P.O. (Travelling Post Office) train from Aberdeen on 25th July 1956. For many a year the T.P.O.'s, with their catching apparatus to collect lineside mail, were very much part of the railway scene. Unfortunately, they have long disappeared. (R. Butterfield)

137) Riddles Austerity War Department Class 8F 2-8-0 No 63077 carried three different numbers during its working life. Apart from LNER No 63077 there was WD No 77277 and finally its BR No 90077. It is seen here in the shed yard at 62B Dundee Tay Bridge on 8th June 1949. This presumably, was its home shed for it was still allocated here in January 1957. Its life was curtailed in May 1963, from 61B Aberdeen (Ferryhill). (A.N.H. Glover)

138) A crowded scene within the cramped confines of the yard outside the straight running shed at 64A St. Margarets (Edinburgh) on 21st June 1953. Nearest the camera is a St. Margarets V3 Class 2-6-2T No 67606 behind which is a sister locomotive and a K3 Class 2-6-0. Despite several moves to different sheds in Scotland No. 67606 ended its days at 64A, being taken out of revenue earning service in December 1962. (R. Butterfield)

73

139)   Equipped with a small snowplough in readiness for the coming winter months, 63D Fort William based J36 Class 0-6-0 No 65237 has the logo of its current owner stencilled on the tender in October 1952 as it stands adjacent to the apparently empty small depot at Mallaig (sub-shed of Fort William) with a trip freight working. Two jibs of cranes raise their arms to the sky as if in salute, between No 65237 and the shed. (R. Butterfield)

140)   Another J36 Class 0-6-0 No 65287 is captured by the camera, this time in the yard at Inveruruie Works on 8th June 1949. Unlike No 65237 in the previous picture No 65287 has a smaller dome and a squat, cut down chimney which does nothing to enhance its external appearance. The allocation of No 65287 is not known on this date, but towards the end of its life it served from 65E Kipps, 65B St. Rollox and 65F Grangemouth. (A.N.H. Glover)

141)   A modern office block and a grim bank of lofty tenement dwellings look down upon 62B Dundee Tay Bridge on a day in August 1962 as a group of youthful spotters share a joke as they wander round the yard, notebooks in hand. One of the numbers which will go into their books is B1 Class 4-6-0 No 61278, a longstanding inmate of Tay Bridge shed. It was taken out of traffic from there in April 1967 when the shed closed. (A.F. Nisbet)

142)   'Right away — but not without me, we are still taking on water supplies'. The friendly driver of V2 Class 2-6-2 No 60835, from 64A St. Margarets (Edinburgh), on express 1X90 special, acknowledges the guard's wave at Hawick on 8th June 1965. The nameplates which once proudly pronounced that No 60835 was named *The Green Howard, Alexandra, Princess of Wales's Own Yorkshire Regiment* had long been stripped off the engine. (Ken Ellis)

143) Pickersgill Caledonian Class 3P 4-4-0 No 54476 (63A Perth) passes Dundee West shed with a local for Dundee from Perth in August 1956. Dundee West shed, of Caledonian Railway vintage, had closed (officially) as a depot (29C) becoming a sub of 62B Tay Bridge. It did, however, continue to house locomotives for many years afterwards. D49 'Shire' Class 4-4-0 No 62728 *Cheshire,* from Tay Bridge, can be seen on the right. (N.E. Preedy)

144) Two Reid designed North British 'Glen' Class 4-4-0's Nos 62493 *Glen Gloy* and 62480 *Glen Fruin* stand in steam next to a wall which is in a less than safe condition which is 'sheltering' the duo inside the shed at which both are based, at 61A Kittybrewster (Aberdeen) on 26th May 1956. Both locomotives were later withdrawn from Kittybrewster, No 62480 (September 1959) and No 62493 (June 1960). (A.N. Glover)

145) Bright summer sunshine envelopes the yard and running shed at the Scottish 'premier' depot of 64B Haymarket in 1958. With not a Pacific in sight smoke curls lazily into the warm air from a trio of locomotives, two of which can be identified as ex. NBR J88 Class 0-6-0T No 68320, a visitor from the not too far away 64A St. Margarets and another former NBR engine, locally based J36 Class 0-6-0 No 65235 *Gough*. (Eric Light)

146) Not long fresh from overhaul WD Class 8F 2-8-0 No 90041, from 61B Aberdeen (Ferryhill), darkens the skyline at Inverurie, near Aberdeen on 6th September 1962 whilst in charge of a pick-up freight. At this stage in time there were six such locomotives based at Ferryhill for the area's heavy freight requirements Nos 90041/77/97, 90455, 90536 and 90640, though No 90455 was withdrawn later in the month. (N.E. Preedy)

147)   An immaculate BR *Clan* Class 4-6-2 No 72002 *Clan Campbell,* from 66A Polmadie (Glasgow), is on foreign territory on 13th September 1959, photographed in the shed yard at 65A Eastfield (Glasgow). Constructed in 1952 *Clan Campbell* was taken out of service at Polmadie in December 1962 after a short working life indeed, mostly from Polmadie. It did, however, have brief flirtations at 64B Haymarket. Scrapping happened at Darlington. (W. Boyden)

148)   Ex. London North Eastern and Great North of Scotland Railways Class D40 4-4-0 No 62242 looks in fine fettle beneath the coaler at Kittybrewster shed, Aberdeen on 8th June 1949. An inside cylinder locomotive from a class first designed in 1899 by W. Pickersgill and built up to 1920. Note the large bogie wheels. No 62242 is from the same class as *Gordon Highlander,* which is preserved. Used for working over most G.N. & S. routes. (A.N.H. Glover)

149)   A beautifully turned out coach is immediately behind this departing view of Pickersgill Caledonian Class 3P 4-4-0 No 54485 (63A Perth) as it pulls away from Bishopbriggs in April 1957 with the 4.37 pm Glasgow (Queen Street) to Perth passenger via Castlecary, Alloa and the Devon Valley line. No 54485 is going the long way home to Perth. (Peter Hay)

150)   An overcast and dreary day at South Leith in Edinburgh on 12th June 1962. WD Class 8F 2-10-0 No 90773, a 65F Grangemouth locomotive, skirts the shoreline with a lengthy mineral train. No 90773 is passing one of its eventual successors in the shape of English Electric Type 1 (later Class 20) No D8076, from 65A Eastfield (Glasgow). No 90773 was withdrawn at the end of 1962 being cut up by Campbells of Shieldhall. (F. Hornby)

151)   With a shunter in close attendance former North British Railway J83 Class 0-6-0T No 68442 marshalls wagons in a weed-strewn yard near to its home shed at 65E Kipps in Glasgow on 27th August 1957. These 1900 designed locomotives were all based in Scotland and used in the main on shunting, station pilot and light freight workings throughout their lives. No 68442 was taken out of service from Kipps in January 1962. (N.L. Browne)

152)   With the sub-shed belonging to 61C Keith in the background, LMS Class 2P 4-4-0 No 40618, a Keith engine, approaches the station at Elgin with a stopping passenger train from Keith on 18th June 1958. Note the Fowler pattern chimney. Transferred to the area from 67B Hurlford in February 1957 to 61B Aberdeen (Ferryhill), No 40618 moved on to the Keith the following month, remaining there until July 1961 before returning to Ferryhill. (F. Hornby)

153)   A small boy, with hands on hips, mixes with a scattering of adults on the overgrown platform at Alva, the terminus of the branch from Cambus, whilst two railwaymen off ex. NBR J36 Class 0-6-0 No 65345 (62A Thornton Junction) are up to their knees in weeds by the tracks on 18th June 1962. No 65345 has just arrived with a joint RCTS/SLS special. The Alva branch had opened in June 1863 and closed on 1st November 1954. (F. Hornby)

154)   A member of the shed staff at 65E Kipps takes a break in the bright sunshine as he rests on a bench in front of a small building in the yard on 27th August 1957. In front of him is a line-up of 'live' steam in the narrow and cramped shed yard. Leading this line-up is McIntosh Caledonian dock shunter Class 2F 0-6-0T No 56172. To the rear of the same is N2/2 Class 0-6-2T No 69518. Both are Kipps engines. (N.L. Browne)

155) Former North British Railway J36 Class 0-6-0 No 65216 *Byng* is hemmed in between two other steam locomotives at 68E Carlisle (Canal) near to the coaling plant in the mid-fifties. Named after one of the Generals famous for their exploits during the Great War, *Byng* was later found working from 66A Polmadie (Glasgow) before moving on to more familiar home territory at 65E Kipps. It was condemned in April 1962. (M.F. Higson)

156) The footplate crew of Gresley J38 Class 0-6-0 No 65934, from 62C Dunfermline, are engaged in conversation as their charge clatters across a cross-over at Alloa with a brakevan in March 1964. A three-wheeled 'plastic pig', registration number SSG 954, and a moped are parked next to a former bay which has had its track removed, part of the rationalisation of every railwayman's 'friend' — Dr. Beeching. (G.W. Sharpe)

157)   Another footplate crew are captured on film having a 'chin-wag', this time at Thornton Junction station on 16th June 1958. Employed on a local freight is 62A Thornton Junction based NBR Reid 'Glen' D34 Class 4-4-0 No 62478 *Glen Quoich,* which has an extended, but rather scorched smokebox. Somebody had taken the trouble to clean the 'lion & wheel' logo on the tender, along with the name and cab number. (F. Hornby)

158)   In 1937 Sir Nigel Gresley introduced six K4 Class 2-6-0's for use on the West Highland line but in 1945 one of their number No 61997 *MacCailin Mor* was rebuilt from a three cylinder loco to a two cylinder one and given the new classification of K1/1 by Thompson. *MacCailin Mor,* from 65J Fort William, is seen in steam at Mallaig shed on 26th May 1959. It was condemned from Fort William at Doncaster Works in June 1961. (A.N.H. Glover)

159)   4-6-0 No 61513 in the yard at Kittybrewster on 8th June 1949 in lined green early BR livery. This S69 4-6-0 was designed by S.D. Holden for the Great Eastern Railway and entered traffic in 1911. The class later became LNER B12 and they were the last inside cylinder 4-6-0's to remain in service on BR. After World War II a number were sent to GNS territory and they were to do fine work from Aberdeen on expresses. (A.N.H. Glover)

160)   62B Dundee Tay Bridge LMS Ivatt Class 2 2-6-0 No 46464 was nicknamed the 'Carmyllie Pilot' because its main duties were shunting the truncated remains of the Forfar to Arbroath via Carmyllie branch. Here it is noted shunting a freight train across the A92 road to the Metal Box Company's works at Elliott Junction, Arbroath on 6th September 1963. Carmyllie station and its counterparts along the branch had closed in 1929. (A.F. Nisbet)

161)	With a wooden station board and a brick built water tower in the background, a filthy LMS Ivatt Class 4 'Flying Pig' 2-6-0 No 43004 awaits departure from Langholm, Dumfries-shire, a former North British Railway branch, with a local to Carlisle on 10th June 1964, where after arrival, it will be despatched to its home shed at 12A Carlisle (Kingmoor) for servicing. The Langholm branch closed to passengers this same year. (F. Hornby)

162)	Tank engine power on show round the exposed turntable at 64A St. Margarets (Edinburgh) on a rain-soaked 25th August 1957. All of the locomotives to be seen are of former North British origin. From left to right are — Y9 Class 0-4-0T No 68102, C16 Class 4-4-2T No 67492, J88 Class 0-6-0T No 68328 (64B Haymarket) and J83 Class 0-6-0T No 68463. The raised signal behind No 67492 is on the main line to Waverley. (N.L. Browne)

163) The 'Royal Branch' at Ballater with its connections for Balmoral, Scottish home of the Royal Family, terminus of the line from Aberdeen, closed in 1966, but on 21st May 1954 it was very much still part of the railway scene with steam firmly in charge. 61A Kittybrewster B1 Class 4-6-0 No 61308, fitted with a small snowplough, awaits departure with an Aberdeen bound local passenger. Note how clean the station and general area is. (F. Hornby)

164) Moving down the line to Aberdeen we find ourselves in the shed yard at 61B Ferryhill on 18th June 1955 where we espy BR Class 5 4-6-0 No 73005, a 63A Perth engine, coupled to an unidentified WD Class 8F 2-8-0. Note that No 73005 has a single line tablet catcher on its cabside. No 73005 moved on to pastures new at 67A Corkerhill (Glasgow) in December 1962 being no longer required at Perth shed. (N.L. Browne)

165) WD Class 8F 2-8-0 No 77313 (90228) in the shed yard at 62A Thornton Junction on 5th June 1949 in company with two ex. NBR J37 Class 0-6-0's and a fellow WD. No 77313 had worked on War Department duty in Belgium, being returned to the UK in 1947. From September 1950 it was allocated to 53E Goole remaining in service there until condemned in September 1963. It was scrapped the same month at Darlington Works. (A.N.H. Glover)

166) Water laps the stonework wall at Fort William station (West Highland line) on 18th June 1960. Gresley K4 Class 2-6-0 No 61995 *Cameron of Lochiel* (62A Thornton Junction) has not long arrived with a Stephenson Locomotive Society special from Glasgow. In the background a former NBR J36 Class 0-6-0 is about to remove the empty stock. Withdrawn in October 1961, No 61995 was cut up at Halbeath Wagon Works, Dunfermline in 1962. (F. Hornby)

167) The west end of Edinburgh (Waverley) station as photographed from the lofty perch above The Mound Tunnel on 11th August 1958. Set to plunge into the 124 yards long tunnel is a local commuter train bound for Fife in the capable hands of D49 Class 'Shire' No 62729 *Rutlandshire,* from 62A Thornton Junction. Today, neither the locomotive nor the 'County' exist, the latter being swallowed up by Leicestershire many moons ago. (T.R. Amos)

168) With steam to spare LMS Class 5 4-6-0 No 44879, a 63A Perth locomotive, approaches the camera at Stonehaven with the down *Granite City* express from Glasgow (Buchanan Street) to Aberdeen on 25th July 1956. When the A4 Pacifics were introduced onto these services, along with other Pacifics in 1962, the timings between the two cities were cut down to three hours, the first time this had been achieved in twenty-three years. (R. Butterfield)

169) Apart from the notorious 'graveyard dump' at 64F Bathgate during the sixties, there were others at Bo'ness, Coatbridge and Lugton all filled with condemned locomotives awaiting despatch to the overworked scrapyards in Scotland. Waiting their turn on 13th April 1963 at Bo'ness are former NBR J83 Class 0-6-0T No 68479 (withdrawn from 65A Eastfield-Glasgow in October 1962) and ex. CR Class 3F 0-6-0 No 57617 (65B St. Rollox in October 1962). (B. Rands)

170) A wooden door stands ajar at the entrance to the small two road shed at Alloa on 5th June 1960. Alloa, a sub-shed of 62C Dunfermline, hosts three former LNER types J38 Class 0-6-0 No 65923, J37 Class 0-6-0 No 64560 and J36 Class 0-6-0 No 65323, all from Dunfermline and out of steam. Alloa shed presumably closed at the same time Dunfermline demised in May 1967. The station closed during 1968. (T.R. Amos)

171) Two Scottish gents observe the passing of BR Class 4 2-6-4T No 80090 as it rattles beneath a wrought iron footbridge at Tayport at the head of the 12.28 pm from Dundee, one of three lunch-time return services on 23rd August 1963. At this stage in time 62B had three of these locomotives (the others being Nos 80123 & 80124) which were the mainstay of the services across the Tay Bridge to Newport and Tayport. (A.F. Nisbet)

172) Another small shed on the Scottish Region is at St. Boswells, a sub of 64F Bathgate on the 'Waverley' route from Carlisle to Edinburgh. Noted in steam in front of the diminutive brick built two road structure on 27th August 1955 is an unidentified J35 Class 0-6-0. By the 'coal stage' is J37 Class 0-6-0 No 64539, from 64G Hawick. Like the locomotives the shed is of North British heritage. (F. Hornby)

173) Whilst remaining on the subject of sub-sheds we find ourselves at Seafield, Edinburgh, a depot which helped to serve the LMS South Leith Dock branch. In its heyday it was quite busy as can be seen in this 1955 photograph of the shed. Facing the camera is an unidentified NBR 0-6-0, whilst on the right are a trio of tank engines including N15 Class 0-6-2's Nos 69130 and 69147 both from the parent shed at 64A St. Margarets. (D.K. Jones)

174) The Glasgow commuters' rush hour is in full swing, and for ex. North British Railway J83 Class 0-6-0T No 68458, from 67A Corkerhill, the day's work is done and it is heading home for servicing and a respite. The scene is at Ibrox where all signals are set for clear on 29th April 1960. No 68458 had been at Corkerhill since February 1960, moving on to 67C Ayr, its final home, in February 1961. (Peter Hay)

175) The locoshed at 61A Kittybrewster was once situated on the west side of the station (closed in 1968) with the top end of the yard visible from the same. It closed to steam around August 1961, some five and a half years before its counterpart at 61B Ferryhill. In the yard at Kittybrewster on 22nd June 1953, with a scorched smokebox, is ex. NBR D34 'Glen' Class 4-4-0 No 62479 *Glen Sheil,* an inmate of the shed. (R. Butterfield)

176) A young spotter dreams of the day that he too might become a steam engine driver as he peers into the cab of Carlisle (Canal) based A3 Class 4-6-2 No 60095 *Flamingo* from a platform at Edinburgh (Waverley) on 20th June 1958. *Flamingo* is in charge of a 'Waverley' route express to Carlisle. Although sporting a 68E shedplate, Canal's code had in fact changed to 12C earlier in the year. A double chimney was fitted to No 60095 in February 1959. (N.L. Browne)

177) Moving down the 'Waverley' route from Waverley this next picture is taken on a sunlit 27th August 1955 åt Hawick. K3 Class 2-6-0 No 61991, an inhabitant of 64A St. Margarets (Edinburgh), another engine with a scorched smokebox, enters the station with a southbound local passenger train. Rendered surplus to requirement from St. Margarets in May 1959, No 61991 was scrapped at Cowlairs Works three months later. (F. Hornby)

178) 64F Bathgate shed in May 1964. By this date in time most of its famous collection of dumped and unwanted LNER Pacifics had been removed from the depot for scrapping leaving smaller engines to take their place. Two condemned former NBR J36 Class 0-6-0's Nos 65307 and 65329 await their inevitable fate in the shed yard. Both had been withdrawn from Bathgate in December 1963, later being disposed of at Arnott Young, Carmyle. (J. Wraithmell)

179) A final view as taken at 61A Kittybrewster on 7th June 1949. Former London North Eastern and Great North of Scotland D41 Class 4-4-0 No 62225, in fine external condition, is at rest in the shed yard. This class, consisting of twenty-six engines which formed the Pickersgill T Class, had 6'1" driving wheels and they were constructed between 1895 and 1898. (A.N.H. Glover)

180) As can be seen, the narrow three road shed at 65E Kipps, in Glasgow, of North British Railway origin, near to Coatbridge Sunnyside station, is hemmed between an industrial complex and the main running lines. Looking east on 17th May 1953 we can observe two former NBR locomotives, an unidentified N15 Class 0-6-2T (on the right) and J36 Class 0-6-0 No 65214 on the left. (F. Hornby)

181)   A former North British locomotive on ex. North British Railway metals at Burntisland on 16th September 1961. 62A Thornton Junction based J37 Class 0-6-0 No 64564 swings tender-first round a headland whilst skirting the Firth of Forth on the Fife coast with a mixed freight which includes two British Petroleum tank wagons. Withdrawn from Thornton in June 1964 No 64564 disappeared at the hands of the Motherwell Machinery Company. (Peter Hay)

182)   Ex. NBR Reid 'Scott' D30 Class 4-4-0 No 62418 *The Pirate*, from nearby 62A Thornton Junction shed, wheels a three coach local past a strange looking collection of upper and lower quadrant signals at Thornton North Junction on 19th July 1955. This class of handsome engines was nearing the end with extinction only five years away. *The Pirate* was condemned from Thornton in August 1959 being cut up at Old Kilpatrick. (D.K. Jones)

183)   Sunlight and shadow on the Waverley route on 29th July 1960. D49 'Shire' Class 4-4-0 No 62744 *The Holderness,* based at 64G Hawick, trundles over a level crossing (controlled) at Longtown, between Carlisle and Riccarton Junction, with a local passenger train. Longtown used to be a junction for a branch to Gretna (NBR) closed in 1915. *The Holderness* was taken out of traffic at Hawick in December 1960. (Derek Singleton)

184)   We end BRITISH RAILWAYS STEAMING ON THE EX. LNER LINES — Volume 2 with a view taken in the shed yard at 64A St. Margarets (Edinburgh) on 4th June 1949, some eighteen months after British Railways had taken over from the LNER in this part of Scotland. K3 Class 2-6-0 No 61911 still carries the logo of its former masters though the cabside number is a BR one. The smokebox number has still not been affixed. (A.N.H. Glover)